The Quakers: The History and Legacy of the Religious Society of Friends

By Charles River Editors

The Quakers' symbol

About Charles River Editors

Charles River Editors is a boutique digital publishing company, specializing in bringing history back to life with educational and engaging books on a wide range of topics. Keep up to date with our new and free offerings with this 5 second sign up on our weekly mailing list, and visit Our Kindle Author Page to see other recently published Kindle titles.

We make these books for you and always want to know our readers' opinions, so we encourage you to leave reviews and look forward to publishing new and exciting titles each week.

Introduction

A 19th century engraving of a Quakers mission house in the Middle East

The Quakers

"I was plain, and would have all things done plainly; for I did not seek any outward advantage to myself." – George Fox

Since its fruition, Christianity has faced an unremitting string of conflicts, critics, and challenges. As the number of Christian converts grew, the growth in clashes on ideologies and control was only natural. In the same vein, more and more of those who called themselves Christians seemed to be straying further and further away from God's light. Drunkenness, heresy, and immorality were on the rise. The Middle Ages was especially rife with rape, incest, adultery, and other obscene sexual behaviors, which were well-recorded by medieval chroniclers. The English scholar, Alcuin, lamented that civilization had become "absolutely submerged under flood of fornication, adultery, and incest, so that the very semblance of modesty is entirely absent."

Towards the 17th century, the Puritan-raised George Fox became increasingly discouraged by the worsening moral conditions of society. George was unable to fill the spiritual void inside of him, until one day, he discovered his inner "Light." Next came the godly visions. George began to preach about the "true" Word of God, and soon, amassed a following – the Religious Society of Friends, later known as the "Quakers."

Few today know much about the Quakers. Whenever the subject of Quakerism slips into conversation, most picture a rosy-cheeked fellow in a simple black overcoat, and a wide brim hat atop his thick, cloud-white hair, inspired by the famous logo of the Quaker Oats company. In spite of the stereotype, Quakers today come in all colors, shapes, and sizes, with the more liberal folk sporting trendy haircuts, tattoos, and various piercings. They call themselves "Friends," a starkly different but very devout following of God. They strive for a world empowered by peace and acceptance, an ambitious mission fueled by diversity, blind to race, gender, or creed.

As amicably harmless as the Friends might appear, there was once a time when being a Quaker was at the very best an instant conviction, and at the very worst a death sentence. Their unorthodox ideals were considered poisonous and potentially dangerous by authorities, who would fight time and time again to stamp out the flames of their movement, but still, they weathered storm after storm. And while the peace-loving followers of Christ were famed for their views of harmony, by no means were they feeble opponents. Not only would they persevere in the face of persecution, theirs is a movement that is so powerful, it stands strong centuries later, with a following more rich and diverse than ever before.

The Quakers: The History and Legacy of the Religious Society of Friends profiles the life of George Fox, examines the origins of Quakerism, and looks at the Quaker utopia the community attempted to establish in Pennsylvania. This book also covers both the praise and criticism the unusually liberal Christian order has attracted over the centuries. Along with pictures of important people, places, and events, you will learn about the Quakers like never before.

The Quakers: The History and Legacy of the Religious Society of Friends
About Charles River Editors
Introduction
   Religious Strife
   Fox and Friends
   Prison, Persecution, and Perspective
   Quaker Women
   Coming to America
   Friction and Foes
   Freedom Fighters
   Modern Quakers
   Online Resources
   Bibliography
Free Books by Charles River Editors
Discounted Books by Charles River Editors

Religious Strife

"There is something of God in every man, let us affirm it more certainly than ever, but surrounded as we are by millions of new-made graves and with the voices of the hungry and the dispossessed in our ears, let us not easily accept the impious hope that the natural goodness of ourselves is sufficient stuff out of which to fashion a better world." - Gilbert H. Kilpack

The prelude to the Quakers' story goes all the way back to the mid-17th century – more precisely, the English Civil War. Unlike most wars, the seed of the war had not been planted by revolutionaries who sought to usurp the throne with their own brand of government. Rather, the discontented public had become piqued by the overbearing religious authority. It would not be long before the brewing tension escalated into violent conflict.

Critics of the monarch were often pointed to the so-called "Divine Right of Kings," which granted monarchs (at the time Charles I) the right to rule by will of God. These kings were supposedly endorsed by God Himself, which might have made sense to the royals but was head-scratching logic for the public. The restless people called for a more equal balance in power between the King and Parliament, which they believed was their only chance of getting their voices heard.

Most of all, religious tensions stemming from longstanding and ongoing conflicts between the Protestants and Roman Catholics had riled up the public. In 1625, the year King Charles I rose to the throne, he married a sharp-nosed and raven-haired Catholic beauty, Henrietta Maria of France. Included in their marriage treaty was a stipulation that allowed Henrietta to practice her faith without persecution. It also ensured that her fellow Catholics could excuse themselves from Anglican services without penalty.

Charles I of England

Henrietta Maria of France

This startled the largely Protestant public, awakening a fear that hit far too close to home. The horrific reign of Queen Mary I was only less than a century ago, and the carnage that resulted in the queen's determination to revert England to Catholicism was still fresh in their minds. In an attempt to wipe out Protestantism in England, the queen burned at least 300 Protestant "heretics" at the stake, becoming the muse to the nickname and urban legend of "Bloody Mary."

Bloody Mary

A few decades later came the Spanish Armada, a bloody and attempted invasion of England spearheaded by the Catholic King Phillip II, but perhaps the most flagrant sign of the seeming Catholic terror was the Thirty Years War, a dreadful conflict the whole of Europe was currently embroiled in at the time, prolonged by warring Catholic and Protestant authorities across the continent.

As time progressed, the dissatisfaction that nonconformists displayed towards their oppressors steadily worsened. In 1633, the Protestant William Laud was promoted to Archbishop of Canterbury to appease the public, but Laud's base of support was limited. The archbishop became infamous for his attempts to instill religious uniformity through the enforcement of The Book of Common Prayer, and for his unabashed disapproval of the Puritans, a more extreme group of reformed Protestants. He would also make a number of changes that incensed the public, including the revival of stained glass windows, exquisitely carved religious statues, and colorful vestments for high-ranking priests. These new changes, many believed, were a conspiracy to secretly squeeze Catholic elements into their lives.

Laud

Tensions with nonconformists reached an all-time high when their freedom of speech was stripped from them. In 1637, a trio of prolific Puritan pamphleteers, William Prynne, Henry Burton, and John Bastwick, were charged with "seditious libel." Their ears were sliced off, and the letters "S.L." were marked onto their cheeks with a blistering-hot branding iron as a reminder of their crimes.

Outright war was close at hand. That same year, when King Charles I attempted to revise the prayer book, the first wave of riots erupted in Edinburgh. The revisions, which many believed reeked of Catholic motives, enraged Scottish Presbyterians, who were now on a mission to take back their freedom of worship. In response, the king simply curbed the riots, the public protests falling on his deaf ears. The king hustled to push the sanctioned prayer book, and made examples of those who refused. The year after, the Scots grudgingly signed a treaty pledging their loyalty to the king. Another year later, the king dispatched an army to inspect the state of worship among the Scottish communities, which irked them even more.

The king's winning streak would taper out by the First and Second Bishop Wars of 1639 and 1640. Unfortunately, the lackluster royal army cost the king both wars, and the infuriated monarch was left with no choice but to sign off on the degrading terms of the Treaty of Ripon. As a result, king was forced to cough up the territories of County Durham and Northumerland. Even more biting, the city of Newcastle was ceded to the Scots, and he was now required to pay £850 (roughly $97,400 USD today) a day to preserve the military there.

Another ingredient that led to the king's fall was the lack of royal funding. His father, King James I, had never been too concerned with money. Before James had become king, he was spoiled by a series of private plays, concerts, and other entertainment noble families enjoyed. As royalty, James believed he deserved the best of the best. Perhaps not surprisingly, James soon picked up a serious spending habit. £25,000 (roughly $3.57 million USD today) in pocket money was set aside every year for the young Prince Henry to splurge as he pleased, while the family shopped frivolously and hosted regular private shows and over-the-top parties with bands and luscious feasts. The average spending for royal clothing climbed from £10,000 ($1.146 million USD) in 1603 to £36,000 ($4.125 million) in 7 years.

A generation later, it was difficult for Charles to tweak his expensive taste, and by the time of his reign, the royal funds were seriously endangered. Charles made things no better, as he was an avid patron and benefactor of the arts who insisted upon purchasing expensive artwork and attending all art-related events with the finest seats in the venue. To keep up his extravagant lifestyle, the royals often sought out loans, but Parliament was especially well-acquainted with the history of the irresponsible finances in the royal family and eventually cut them off. This lack of funding resulted in ill-equipped and under-trained royal forces.

On August 22, 1642, civil war was officially declared, one that would rage on for 9 years straight. With the help of the Puritan Oliver Cromwell, Parliament would win the war, but when Cromwell died in 1658, Charles' son, Charles II, would make his way to the throne, 3 years later.

Cromwell

Charles II of England

Like his father, Charles II seemed to have learned little from his family's notorious tradition of unnecessary spending. He continued that reckless lifestyle, and was soon dubbed the "Merry Monarch," fabled for his unforgettable parties, constant circles of women, and endless booze consumption.

Meanwhile, the Anglican bishops Charles II had appointed took the driver's seat on national matters, once again hoping to bring back the religious uniformity that Laud had once fought for. In 1662, the Act of Uniformity was issued, which called for all the churches in England to abide by the same set of prayers, ceremonies, and sacrament administration according to The Book of Common Prayer. All ministers, pastors, and religious leaders, regardless of sect, were made to sign an oath that prohibited them from straying from the good book and "endeavor[ing] any change or alteration of government, either in church or state."

The 24th of August was marked on every calendar that year. This was the deadline for all tithes, rents, and other taxes, which would be submitted to the royal clergy. Ministers that protested were promptly kicked off their posts and had their payments withheld. However, this was the day determined nonconformists decided to take a stand; over 2,000 ministers, about 20% of the population, were expelled from the Church of England. The displaced nonconformists were scattered across the continent and driven underground, but they were continuously hunted by church-sanctioned spies. Those who were caught were dragged back to authorities, and severely punished.

It was this very expulsion that gave birth to the golden age of dissenters, who had long been practicing their religions behind sealed doors. They were the Presbyterians, the Congregationalists, the Unitarians, the Baptists, and the Quakers. Authorities had hoped that the crackdown would quicken their extinction, but it soon became clear that the effect was anything but.

Fox and Friends

"Why should any man have power over any man's faith, seeing Christ Himself is the author of it?" – George Fox, as quoted in "Memoirs of George Fox"

In July of 1624, in a small Puritan village known as Drayton-in-the-Clay, just a few miles from Leicester, a cooing baby George was welcomed into the Fox household. George was the oldest of 4 children in a middle class family, born to Christopher Fox, a weaver by trade, and his wife, Mary Lago.

A plaque commemorating Fox's birthplace

A portrait believed to depict Fox

Unlike the dark pasts shared by some of history's most influential figures, George, raised in a Puritan household, had a relatively comfortable childhood. That said, some uncertainty still exists as to what George Fox was truly like, as his image is one only memorialized in centuries-old paintings. George was often depicted as a broad-faced man with wide, hawk-like eyes and a prominent, beak-like nose.

Another depiction of Fox

Presumably, these features must have been even more striking on a child, but beyond that, George had always known that he was nothing like his peers. Like many boys his age, George learned to read and write, but little is known about his formal education. What was widely known was his intrigue with God and religion at an early age, as well as his observant disposition, which seemed to be beyond his years. At the age of 11, he exhibited an obsession in living a life of "pureness and righteousness." While other children busied themselves with games and socializing with their friends, George was said to have been deconstructing the Lord's word and applying it to his daily interactions. The self-aware George described his experience in his autobiography, writing, "I had a gravity and stayedness of mind and spirit, not usual in children."

George was also unusually comfortable on his own as a child, and he displayed a self-professed commitment to brutal honesty. Since these were anomalous traits for a child, George became subject to relentless bullying by his peers. Rather than fight back, George seemed to be more curious about the source of the mockery, and never engaged them in physical retaliation, adopting a philosophy of let go and let be.

Those around George had always predicted that he would one day join the priesthood, but to everyone's surprise, he neglected that seemingly obvious path. Instead, he spent the latter half of his youth as the apprentice to a shoemaker and pastoral farmer, George Gee, who hailed from the village of Mancetter. The young man was a fast learner, and he was frequently commended by customers and coworkers for his professionalism and honesty.

George would also later serve a short stint as a shepherd, but his career shift would prove to be a pivotal one. As he steered the flocks of bleating sheep across the lush green pastures, the still of nature cast its spell on him. He peeled his eyes open to the significance of embracing the beautiful simplicity of life, free from luxury and material pleasures. While he kept himself clean, he abandoned popular grooming trends and donned plain clothing to express his newfound appreciation for modesty. Moreover, as the naturally perceptive George grew older, the blindfolds of hypocrisy slowly came undone. His peers, acquaintances, and even his own family declared themselves followers of Christ, but their lives outside of church were bristling with binge-drinking, gambling, and other debauchery.

All it took was one event to rock 19-year-old George's world. In the summer of 1643, George visited a local fair with one of his cousins, where the pair met up with some mutual friends. When the festivities began to wind down, the group decided to stop at a nearby bar for a quick pint. George had never been much of a drinker, but not wanting to dampen the mood, he took them up on their offer, and ordered a glass for himself. Within seconds, the rowdy group had knocked back their first glasses and were thumping the counters with their fists, hollering for another round. They had planned on returning to the festival, but the tipsy men were now challenging each other to a drinking game. Whoever refused to drink, they announced, would be responsible for all their tabs at the end of the night.

George's hot ears rang with disbelief. How dare these men be so bold as to suggest such a thing? Not even his non-Christian acquaintances had ever ventured such a hedonistic act. The man of few words, as always, had little to say. He simply paid for his drink and exited the pub, feeling lost and dejected. That night, George paced round and round in his room, his insomnia triggered by the spiritual labyrinth he had inadvertently stumbled into. He negotiated for hours with God through prayer and silent reflection, begging for answers to the questions flooding his mind. In the midst of his prayer fest, an internal voice that he believed came from God spoke to him. The voice proclaimed, "You see how young people go together into frivolity, and old people into the earth; you must leave all, young and old, keep out of all, and be as a stranger to all."

A part of George was hesitant about leaving behind a family he so dearly loved, but God's message was loud and clear, and it was one that could not be ignored. A few months later, George packed up his essentials and left the cozy town. For years, he roamed, flitting from one religious sect to the next, in pursuit of the truth behind the word of God.   George's deep depression was laden over a simmering existential crisis, which made for a tough journey, and was made even more difficult with the volatile background of the civil war. First, he found himself in Barnet, a market town by London. As a young male, George, only human, felt the enticements of the temptations that lay in the neighboring resort town. To repel these temptations, he either shuttered himself in his room or took extensive walks in the calming countryside, finding a friend in nature.

After about a year, George returned home for a quick visit. He reunited with some relatives and friends, who urged him to take a wife or join the military to lay his problems to rest. The deflated George rejected the advice thrust in his direction, and grew even more saddened by their inability to understand the root of his problems.

It was during this same trip that George reacquainted himself with Nathaniel Stephens, a local clergyman who had always enjoyed religious debates and general banter with the bright young man. Upon George's return, however, Stephens quickly choked back his praises as the pair began to clash in bitter disputes over Christian ideologies. When George disrupted one of Stephens' lectures, the clergyman painted him barking "mad," and the disgraced George was pelted with stones and forcefully ejected from his hometown.

Over the next 4 years, George continued his search for a solution to his spiritual distress, vigorously hounding an assortment of clergymen from various sects and backgrounds. During the turbulent ride, he kept his Bible close at hand, scanning page after page of Scripture for enlightenment. He encountered a wide range of religious experts who aimed to help him overcome his spiritual unease, only to be met with one failure after another. For example, one minister from Warwickshire advised him to incorporate tobacco and psalm-singing into a ritualistic ceremony, but George did not care for it. Another clergyman suggested bloodletting, the antiquated process of extracting blood as a means to alleviate physical and psychological ailments. Legend had it that not a blood of drop could be extracted from George, as he was completely drained from the spiritual emptiness inside of him.

In Coventry, a city in the West Midlands of England, George began to consult with a highly reputable clergyman and physician known as Dr. Cradock. One day, as Cradock led his students around a stroll around his prized garden, George came close to slipping. In the process, George trampled on one of the doctor's beloved flowers, which sent Cradock flying into such a rage that it was as if "his house had been on fire." Once again, George was cast aside, even more damaged than he was before. Months later, George attempted to mingle with a new group of dissenters, but he was soon labeled a pariah for asserting that women possessed souls of their own.

To most, the bleak years of dead ends might have been a sign to wrap it up and head on home with their tails between their legs, but quitting was simply absent from his DNA. George spent his days fasting and meditating, and his nights on quiet walks or snuggled up against a tree, armed only with a Bible. It was during this period of intense self-reflection that it slowly dawned on him – he could not associate himself with Christians who were not truly living in Christ's light. Finally, he decided that if he had to do this on his own, so be it.

From that point on, the obstacles of George's spiritual quest seemed to evaporate, and he began to chance upon the very answers he had been searching for the entire time. Though he was still physically present on Earth, George claimed that he had now elevated himself to a higher dimension, one that had seen the Kingdom of God. Only 2 paths existed that would bring one to the Heavenly Kingdom – one that was rampant with death and despair, and the other with pure love and light, which would ultimately lead them to God's side. An excerpt from George's journal reads, "I was taken up in the love of God...it was opened to me by the eternal light and power...and I...clearly saw that all was done and to be done in and by Christ, and how He conquers and destroys this tempter, the devil, and all his works..."

These "openings," as George called them, provided the process of understanding what it took to walk on the path of purity, its instructions divulged to him in a chain of fully-realized revelations. Based on George's divine disclosures, Jesus Christ was the Holy Light that inspired and enlightened all of mankind, and the secret to understanding Him could be unlocked within oneself. If one were to listen closely and serve the Lord without grievances, they, too, could be transformed by the Light, and made pure in the name of Christ.

In addition to these openings, George was said to have been blessed with divine, magical powers, including the resurrection of the dead. His enlightenment also gifted him with psychic-like abilities, and he had allegedly predicted a number of English disasters and war victors with chilling accuracy, such as the Great Fire of London. He even foretold the assassinations of many famous folk, including his own, thereby dodging his own would-be deaths on multiple instances.

George had heard his calling – it had become his mission to spread the word about his new revelations.

Prison, Persecution, and Perspective

"The Lord showed me, so that I did see clearly, that he did not dwell in these temples which man had commanded and set up, but in people's hearts...his people were his temple, and he dwelt in them." – George Fox

In 1648, 24-year-old George began to preach to the masses. Day after day, George camped out in bustling marketplaces and "steeple houses," which were the less-frequented topmost floors of old church towers. It appeared as if George's enlightenment had reshaped him completely. Now that he had been illuminated by the Holy Spirit, he more than stepped out of his shell, and began to reel people in with his charm, eloquence, and gospel.

George had only intended to indoctrinate the public about what he believed were the true principles of Christianity, and he was not necessarily looking for followers, but he soon amassed a fraction of the public who had become enchanted by his religious zeal. These followers, perhaps influenced by the ideas of the then-budding Age of Enlightenment, began to question traditional religion, and they were naturally drawn to George's refreshing views on tolerance and righteousness. They clung on to his every word and beseeched him to teach them about the "openings," and how to discover the Light within. In time, they began to call themselves the "Children of the Light," or the "Friends of Truth," which would later be shortened to just "Friends." Together, the Friends began the lifetime process of "silent waiting" for the all-healing and all-knowing Light.

George's popularity among lost dissenters began to thrive, so much so, that whenever the man was scheduled to arrive in a new town, a horde of loyal followers would already be there to greet him. Some praised him for his proficiency in deciphering the obscurest of Scriptures. Some were mesmerized by his divine magic, with witnesses claiming that entire buildings convulsed during George's most powerful sermons. The tense religious climate made it easy for George to pick apart competing religious divisions, which won him even more followers.

Of course, the newly charismatic George had not lost his penchant for challenging public norms and ideals, and soon the authorities caught wind of the troubling character. George had become known for slamming several religious and civil requirements, such as tithes, insisting they were snuck into the pockets of corrupt landlords. He campaigned for the release of criminals he deemed had been imprisoned unjustly, humiliating the authorities. Most pressing of all was the steel-like persistence of George and his Friends; as they roved from town to town, preaching their peculiar views, they would encounter ferocious naysayers who whipped, battered, and chased them out of their lands. Nonetheless, they remained cool and undeterred.

In 1649, George would finally pay the first major price for his insolence. On his way to a meeting with Friends in Nottingham, God had apparently invigorated him with the need to "go and cry against yonder great idol and the worshipers there within." Heeding God's message, he took a detour and stopped at a church along the way. There, he sat in the pews for some time, before the Light ignited within him a second time. He shot up from his seat and denounced the preacher for his "scriptural errors." Before he could finish his tirade, church members hooked their arms under his and flung him out of the premises. An hour later, he was sitting in a jail cell.

George was released from prison about a month later, but this was far from his last stay in the slammer. It was the first time he had ever been thrown behind bars, but he remained undaunted, the Light in him glowing brighter than ever. On the day of his release, he traveled to the next town, and took a seat in the back pew of the local church. This time, George had requested for a guest spot in the pulpit at the end of the service, but as soon as he took to the podium and relayed his revelations, the crowd broke out in murmurs and gasps. Before he could retreat, he was seized, beaten, ensnared in stocks, and marched right out of town by an angry mob. This was not the first or last time he would be driven out of town, but he carried on.

In 1650, George, now 26, trekked to Twy-Cross in Leicestershire with 2 companions. The three were in terrible spirits as they made their way through markets, fairs, and faceless crowds, seeing nothing but "death and darkness in all the people, where the power of God had not shaken them." Still, they continued their journey, with George's internal compass leading them to the city of Derby, south of Derbyshire. There, as his companions snoozed on the hard floors in the home of one of his fans, he heard the distant ringing of a church bell. Taking his cue, George shook his companions awake and took them towards the steeple house.

George was elated to see that almost all of the important men in town were present, including high-ranking officials in the army and priesthood. Once he was kissed by the Holy Spirit, George began to preach to them. Instead of the usual uproar he had grown accustomed to, he was met with crickets and uncomfortable silence. When the crowd recovered, George and his companions were gently taken away and presented to the local magistrate. All 3 were convicted on the charge of blasphemy. One of George's companions quickly recanted his statements and was discharged, while George and the other were sentenced to half a year in prison.

While in captivity, George claimed that numerous thinkers and learned men in society had paid him a visit for spiritual guidance, but none compared to the turnaround from the prison's own warden. Initially, the warden had hated George with a passion, lambasting him as a renegade and "speaking wickedly" about the prisoner. That was, until the Lord decided to smite the warden with a vision of his own. One day, George had apparently overheard the warden confiding in his wife. The warden whispered, "I have seen the day of judgment, and I saw George there; and I was afraid of him, because I have done him so much wrong, and spoken so much against him to the ministers, professors...justices, and in taverns and ale houses." Later that night, the sheepish warden was said to have entered George's cell, and personally apologized to him. George immediately forgave him, but the warden, who was deeply ashamed, declared that he could not have George as his prisoner in good conscience, so he spent the night on the floor of George's cell.

The next morning, George appeared before a certain Justice Bennet, one of the Friends' most venomous critics. It was this day that Bennet christened them "Quakers" for the first time, for he had heard many stories about how George "bade [his followers] tremble at the word of the Lord." It had been meant as an insult, but the name would ultimately stick.

In the months after, rabbles of George's admirers continued to pester the court about his release, with some even offering hefty sums for his freedom. The exhausted magistrate adjusted his sentencing and permitted him to exit the prison during scheduled hours, during which he was allowed to roam freely so long as he stayed within a 1-mile radius. George sensed that the magistrate had been hoping that he would "disappear" on one of his walks. He later confronted a guard, who confirmed his suspicions. In response, George merely said that he was not one to fright and flee, especially if he had done nothing wrong.

A few weeks later, George was presented before Justice Bennet once again. The judge informed George that if he took responsibility for his crime of blasphemy, he would be free to leave. Yet again, jaws dropped as George politely refused the offer. Bennet supposedly flared up and slapped him across the face, but George forgave him publicly and returned to his cell, serving the full 6 months of his sentence.

George was ultimately released, but his freedom was short-lived. By now, he had accumulated so many devotees that several new recruits in the local army refused to have anyone other than George as their commander. The magistrate promoted George to captaincy, but the man shrugged off the title. The incandescent Bennet hurled him back into prison, hoping to change his mind by housing him with the worst prisoners available. Without batting an eye, George made himself comfortable in his new home, ministering whenever he could to his new cellmates and answering letters to those on the outside. Eventually, when it became clear that George could not be broken, he was set free in 1651.

For the next 12 months, George picked up where he had left off and restarted his mission, accompanied by a select group of the most passionate Friends. The triumphs and failures of the meetings they held along the way were a constant gamble, but every destination on their agenda was crossed off. Unlike the Jesuits and many other Christian factions, the Quakers did not beg for money, as they believed in self-sustenance, whether it be spiritual or superficial.

George's attempt at evangelizing the tiny town of Tickhill had been one of his biggest flops. In the middle of his sermon, one of the local clergymen lunged forth and whacked him across the face with a Bible with such vehemence that buckets of blood gushed out of George's nose. The local magistrate offered to arrest the man, but George declined to press charges, forgave his attacker, and went on his way.

A few months later, as George stood on the crown of Pendle Hill, he was struck with yet another vision from above. The divine imagery displayed a sea of people in flawless-white garb, "coming to the Lord." Now convinced that he was destined to realize this vision, he continued to hike across the country.

Firbank Fell, a charming hill resting snugly between the towns of Sedbergh and Kendal, would become home to one of his most tremendous success stories. These faraway towns tucked away in the northwestern corner of England had been neglected by religious authorities, its citizens written off as uncivilized "back country" bumpkins. While most were indeed less educated, they possessed a rare open-mindedness and fire for learning. Soon, a group of Seekers was formed, all committing to preach the Quaker-approved gospel of the Lord. They were divided and tasked with taking on different regions of England, bearing with them the Quaker message of love, peace, and Christian goodness. These new followers became known as the "Valiant Sixty," its membership including names such as the nonconformist Francis Howgill; James Nayler, a radical but enthusiastic character; and George Whitehead, one of the few teenagers in the following. As a unit, the Quakers became collectively known as the "Religious Society of Friends."

The Valiant Sixty, along with the rest of the Friends, were instructed to abide by the Testimony of Simplicity. In essence, the Quakers embraced living a modest and uncomplicated life. They urged one another to focus on what was essential in life – one's spirituality and character, as opposed to trivial material pleasures or status, as they damaged the foundations of the bridge linking one to God. And while there were no official uniforms, Quakers were famed for their adherence to a "plain" dress code. Flamboyant fabrics and designs were seen as a sign of social inequality, and thus were considered wasteful and narcissistic. Today, most Quakers no longer wear old-fashioned coats, tunics, or plain dresses but prefer basic and watered-down versions of modern clothing. They avoid designer labels and opt for fairly simple fashion.

The Friends were also required to practice simplicity in speech. George instructed his followers to address one another with the humble terms of "thee" or "thou," rather than "you," which was reserved for the most dignified names in society. Though this was intended to promote equality among Quaker brothers and sisters, outsiders took offense to this, deeming it a sign of disrespect.

The element of simplicity was practiced in all other areas of Quaker life. That established, Quakers may have disregarded wealth, but remained firm that poverty was separate from, and in turn, did not affect one's spiritual character. The more affluent Quakers were not required to give away all their riches and possessions, but could not flaunt their wealth. In a letter George authored during the latter years of his life, he confirmed that membership was open to people of all backgrounds, educated or uneducated. After all, many of the Bible's own leading men, such as Moses and Noah, had once been lowly shepherds.

The Quakers rebuffed the widely-held Protestant belief of "sola scriptura," which claimed that the Holy Book was the written word of God. Instead, George and his followers insisted that Christ Himself was the word of God. As much as George cherished his Bible, the Scripture, he believed, was a reference book but not a rule book, as God has never "dwell[ed] in a temple made with hands." Needless to say, outsiders clutched their pearls at the very thought of this principle.

George did not leave a specific creed or handbook for the Quakers, but those who followed him knew the Quaker aims and principles by heart. Friends lived a life shaped by integrity, honesty, humility, moral purity, and Christian goodness, and promised never to turn down anyone who sought their help. There were no special ceremonies or weekly services that Quakers were required to attend, other than a Monthly, Quarterly, and a Yearly Meeting. Meetings varied between Quaker communities, but in most cases, Friends sat in silence until they felt an internal "provocation" to share a testimony.

The Quakers were no less pious than the average Christian, but they found no use for traditional Christian sacraments. Baptism was not required as a rite for a seat in the membership, and special meals among Friends were considered worthy of communion. Most Quaker communities do not prohibit lavish ceremonies, but they are frowned upon, as it is generally believed that spiritual experience should be derived from one's bond with God.

Many found the Quaker ideals fresh and exhilarating, but authorities were appalled by these "toxic" practices. The vision on Pendle Hill had unfettered George of any iota of doubt that remained in his system. In less than 3 years, Quaker venues hosted by George and his followers attracted over a thousand attendees each time. It was at this point that authorities began to seriously regard the Quakers as a serious threat. Some accused them of witchcraft, and others of conspiring to overthrow the government. Authorities decided to nip the problem in the bud before it spread, and in 1655, George was arrested in Whetstone Village and sent to London.

In London, George was taken to Oliver Cromwell, a prestigious name in the English military, and the Lord Protector of the Commonwealth of England. After an unusually calm and civil conversation, George assured Cromwell that the Quakers had no interest in the government. By the end of their talk, Cromwell, too, was allegedly so moved by his words that his eyes welled up with tears at the time of George's departure. Cromwell vowed to welcome his new friend into his home at any time.

Throughout 1656, George and Cromwell exchanged a series of letters. George pleaded with Cromwell to relax the restrictions against Quakers, but Cromwell, who had his hands tied, declined to help. Even so, the pair would hold a few more meetings in the next 2 years until Cromwell's death in 1658.

Around the same time, George would come across one of the earliest examples of internal conflict with James Nayler, the most rash and outspoken of all the Valiant Sixty. The pair butted heads rather frequently, as Nayler often abandoned protocol, including instances that saw him refusing to kiss George's hand and removing his hat during prayer. Nayler was also something of a mischief-maker, and he was even jailed during one of George's imprisonments. When Nayler was released, he stirred the pot once more when he trotted into Bristol on a horse, tailed by a line of stripping followers who chanted the words "Holy, holy, holy" over and over again. No one other than Nayler appreciated his homage to Palm Sunday, and he was swiftly charged with blasphemy. He came close to a death sentence, but he was spared in the last minute. As punishment, he was whipped and beaten on a parade from Bristol to London, after which the letter "B" (for blasphemer) was stamped on his forehead. After 3 years of hard labor and solitary confinement, Nayler reunited with George and asked for his forgiveness. Not long after the peace-making, Nayler was ambushed by thieves and left for dead.

The Quakers' outlandish ideas continued to incite outcries and chaos, and as a result, were continuously persecuted throughout the centuries. They were overtly targeted with a series of bans and restrictions. The first was the "Quaker Act of 1662," which made it punishable by law to refuse the Oath of Allegiance to the royal crown. Those who objected were banned from hosting secret meetings.

The Quakers paid the new decree no mind, as they did not care for "superficial oaths." 2 years later, the decree was reaffirmed in the "Conventicle Act of 1664," which reiterated punishment for those who rejected the oath. Despite these laws, the Quakers went on to preach in open forums and public spaces.

Quaker Women

"I do the secret work of God going on in people's minds. Look not at the hard rocks, nor look not at the briars, nor look not at the thorns...for the true seeds-men must not regard weather, the winds that blow; they sow the seed before the winter." – Margaret Fell, wife of George Fox

1652 was perhaps the most momentous year of George's life. Shortly after his vision, he would meet his one true love: Margaret Fell, who was 10 years his senior and would one day be hailed as the "Mother of Quakerism."

An etching depicting Margaret

Born "Margaret Askew," Margaret walked down the aisle for the first time at the age of 18 when she married a renowned British lawyer by the name of Thomas Fell. Once the wedding bells tolled, she became the Lady of Swarthmoor Hall, a handsome 3-story Elizabethan mansion built with limestone and decorated with sleek oak paneling. In the years that followed, she had 9 children by him. Thomas became a judge, as well as an influential member of Parliament, but he would later resign when Oliver Cromwell came into the picture.

When Margaret wandered into the crowd before George at Firbank Fell, she was still married to Thomas. She, like those around her, was bewitched by George's impassioned rhetoric. Though she was hopelessly smitten, she remained faithful to her husband. Still, aiming to make a difference in the movement, Margaret offered the spacious accommodation of Swarthmoor Hall, which would become the main Quaker headquarters.

SWARTHMORE HALL.

A contemporary depiction of Swarthmoor Hall

For the next 6 years, Margaret volunteered as a secretary of sorts, serving directly under her idol, George. Day in and day out, she spent her time sorting the letters they received from the Valiant Sixty ministers on tour, and her drive would not go unnoticed. She was later entrusted with the responsibility of responding to letters, as well as creating epistles of her own.

Meanwhile, Thomas had also fallen victim to his wife's infectious spirit, and took quite a liking to Quakerism. His support for the movement was said to have been the cause of his drop in professional popularity towards the end of his life.

After Thomas's death in 1658, Margaret was granted sole ownership of the mansion. It continued to act as the Quaker headquarters, and also became a refuge for Quakers and other dissenters. Word soon spread about the haven for heathens, and towards the 1660s, Swarthmoor Hall became a target for unannounced government raids and inspections.

Margaret, one of the Valiant Sixty, certainly played a crucial role in paving the path for the early Quaker movement. Whenever George or another Friend was arrested, it was nearly always unanimously decided that Margaret would be sent to negotiate with the persecution on their behalf. She was also tasked with writing the Quakers' first public declaration of a peace treaty in a pamphlet entitled, "A Declaration and an Information from Us, the People Called Quakers, to the Present Governors, The King and Both Houses of Parliament, and All Whom It May Concern." The pamphlet outlined the Quakers' principles in detail, and made a firm call for their religious freedom – sadly, to no avail.

In 1664, 50-year-old Margaret was arrested during one of the raids in Swarthmoor Hall for holding illegal meetings. Like George, Margaret kept her cool, and she was prepared to serve all 6 months of her sentence. The fearless woman claimed that "as long as the Lord blessed [her] with a home, [she] would worship Him in it." On account of her supposed lack of remorse, exasperated authorities extended her sentence to lifetime imprisonment and ordered for the immediate confiscation of Margaret's property.

Margaret was determined not to let her days in confinement go to waste, and she began to counsel her fellow prisoners. In her down time, she churned out a series of books about Quakerism. One of her most celebrated works, Womens Speaking Justified, highlighted the prejudice against women in society, as well as their roles and contributions to the Quaker ministry.

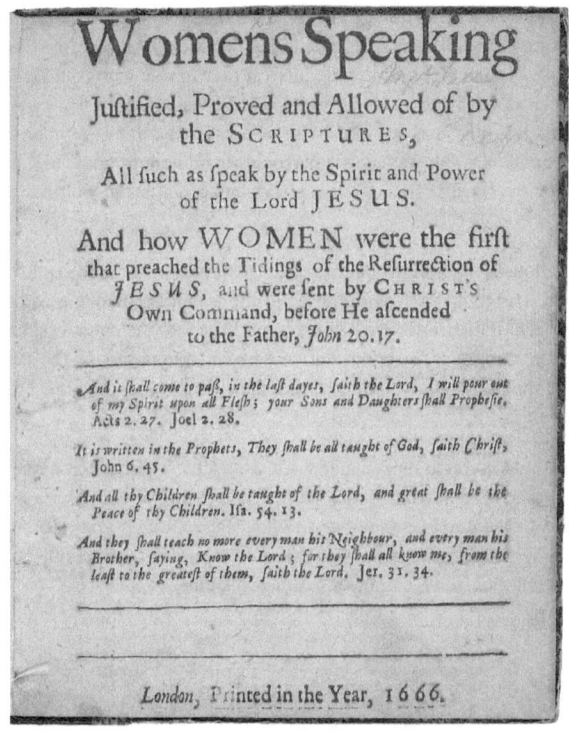

The title page of a 1666 edition of Women's Speaking Justified

She was eventually released in 1668. The year after, Margaret and the 44-year-old George could no longer suppress the chemistry between them, and they confessed their love for one another. Later that year, they were married.

The Quakers not only accepted female members into their ministry; in fact, in a time when women were considered an inferior class, undeserving of a vote or a voice in public forums, the Quakers saw them as equals. From the very beginning of George's Quaker career, he disregarded the haughty snorts around him and invited dozens of women on board, to the extent that some believed women made up the majority of the first Friends. Apart from Margaret, some of the earliest female members included Mary Fisher, Elizabeth Hooten, and Sarah Fell, George's stepdaughter. As soon as these women received their calling, they traveled to various towns, attending monthly meetings, praying with families, and mingling with the public.

Sarah Fell was known for her exquisite beauty and shapely figure, but she is most remembered for her generous soul, especially when it came to her patience for the needy. She loaned poor families money with a much more affordable interest rate. Those who could not scrounge up the cash were not punished, but were instead forgiven, and considered charity cases. Because of Sarah's benevolent spirit, it is said that almost all of debts owed to her were repaid. Sarah was also a gifted mathematician, and served as a personal accountant to many of Quaker friends. She would later headline the construction of a local bank and grammar school in the town of Ulverston.

The first meetinghouses featured wooden partitions that divided the male and female Quakers. In 1671, George decided to do away with those partitions and decided that women would have a private place to preach of their own. He had taken into account the countless times men interjected and seized control of the conversation when a woman was on the stand. Not only did he want to train the quieter women on how to find their own voices, he hoped to sharpen all their skills as public speakers for future missions.

Quaker women would go on to make a name for themselves. There was a rise in female writers who shared profound ideas that were well-received by the public, such as the works of abolitionists Elizabeth Margaret Chandler and Lydia Maria Child. Sybilla Righton Masters, widely considered the first American woman inventor, would become another to shatter the glass ceiling when she revolutionized a cornmeal making machine.

Lydia Child

A number of Quaker martyrs were also women. Rival sects were revolted by the Quakers' inclusion of women, particularly Puritan ministers, and Mary Barrett Dyer, an American Quaker, would be one of the first to feel the burn of their wrath. Mary had heard about 3 of her Quaker friends who were locked up in a Boston prison, where Quakerism was outlawed. When she stopped by for a visit, Mary was chucked into prison alongside them. The 4 were later released under the condition that they never return to Boston, but the defiant Mary returned a month later, packing vengeance. The Boston authorities, proving to be men of their word, had her hanged.

19th century depictions of Mary Dyer being led to the gallows

3 other unnamed Quaker women from England would meet a similarly bold but grisly fate in Dover, New Hampshire. These women, who would also be arrested for blasphemy, were soon

captured by authorities. Their tops were then torn off, and their bare backs were lashed as a snickering priest purportedly looked on. When these women were set free, they built a church in Dover. Centuries later, over a third of Dover's population consisted of Quakers.

Despite the red-hot target on their backs, the Quakers expanded across the continent. They succeeded in gaining followings in Ireland, the Netherlands, Norway, Switzerland, and even Russia. By the time of George's death in 1691, there were an estimated 50,000 Quakers around the globe.

Coming to America

"Sense shines with a double luster when it is set in humility. An able yet humble man is a jewel worth a kingdom." – William Penn

Exactly 20 years after the birth of George Fox, another Quaker legend was born.

William Penn was the son of a London-based admiral, Sir William Penn, Sr., who had been knighted by King Charles II. He had always been aware of the fantastic shoes that he had to fill. His father was among the most esteemed members of British society, praised for his service in the Navy during the Civil War. As a reward for the man's services, Oliver Cromwell presented him with several estates in Ireland. As much as others revered his father, young William never clicked with the man, and the admiral was frequently away at sea, further straining their relationship.

Sir William Penn, Sr.

Throughout his childhood and his college years, William reluctantly attended a sequence of intensely conservative Anglican institutions. He constantly rebelled in an effort to wriggle free from the oppressive chokehold of their strict doctrines, which included the unmovable ban on controversial, ungodly literature, such as the plays of William Shakespeare. Not unlike George, the rebellious young William failed to fit in with his peers.

Before the age of 5, William had contracted smallpox. His hair fell out in clumps until there remained no more. To blend in, he was made to wear a scratchy wig until his post-college years, which did him no favors with his schoolmates. Nonetheless, he learned to embrace his solitude and began to show an interest in the sport of foot-racing. Every day, as soon as class was dismissed, William burst out of his seat and sprinted the full 3 miles home.

William's candid and vociferous nature landed him in hot water multiple times, soon earning him a reputation as a fierce Anglican opponent. These traits followed him into his early adulthood. He was expelled from the Christ Church college (now University of Oxford), for his harsh criticism of the Church of England. A mortified Sir William sent his son away to France.

When 20-year-old William returned to England, he preoccupied himself with a few law courses.

Quakerism had always appealed to William. He was first exposed to the Quakers at age 11 on a trip with his mother to the Netherlands, where he witnessed the awful treatment and persecution of Quakers firsthand. These morbid images left an indelible impression on him. Moreover, William was fascinated by the Quakers' simplicity, as well as their unwavering advocacy for world peace and wholesome Christian living. He, too, was disgusted by the immoral depravity that surrounded him, labeling them "false Christians."

When he turned 21, he was tasked with resolving some business with his father's property in Ireland. It was there that he would formally cross paths with the Quakers for the first time. William soon formed a rapport with the Quakers. He was fully educated on the dangers of associating with the outlawed following, but continued to attend their meetings in Cork, anyway. A year later, he was arrested in a meeting bust. Authorities swiftly recognized him and attempted to reason with him. William was given the chance to sever ties with the Quakers, which was all it took for his release. The 22-year-old resisted, and he decided this would be the perfect opportunity to publicly declare himself a Quaker for the very first time.

William Penn as a young adult

Frederick S. Lamb's painting of a young William Penn

The young man continued to defend the Quakers from his jail cell until he was eventually released thanks to his father. Sir William summoned his son at once and implored him to renounce his heretical faith, but William would not budge. The admiral began to fret about his seemingly unstable child and his radical views; William appeared hell-bent on awakening a rebellion against the monarch, which was sure to deliver to him a fate worse than imprisonment. With a heavy heart, Sir William tossed his son into the streets and canceled his inheritance.

Sir William had hoped that the cruelty of the streets would bring his prodigal son back home, but his son's homelessness only seemed to spark a fire under him. Young William kept his chin up and took up odd jobs, crashing on the floors of various Quaker households until he could find something permanent. It was during this time that William kindled a deep and earnest friendship with George Fox himself. The pair became inseparable, with William tagging along on George's various trips throughout England and Ireland.

4 years later, in 1670, William was reacquainted with the dank and squalid quarters of a jail cell, charged with insubordination against the Church. Sir William, now on his deathbed, was so taken with his son's unbreakable will that he reached out to James, the Duke of York. The dying father cast his pride aside and requested William's release, as well as his son's guaranteed

immunity from religious persecution.

At this stage, Charles II had yet to fulfill a debt owed to Sir William to compensate him for his services during the English-Dutch War, so when the admiral passed on, the ownership of the debt transferred to his son. In 1680, the king chose to honor this debt by offering William a colony in North America, a glorious region next to the Delaware River that spanned 45,000 square miles.

William's mind raced with the potential bursting out of the opportunity presented to him, and, wasting no time, he pounced on the deal. It now became his ambition to start a colony like no other from scratch, fill it with Quakers and religious refugees, and create a utopia of brotherhood and harmony. This became the ultimate goal – one he fondly dubbed "The Holy Experiment." William proposed the name of "Sylvania," or Latin for "woods," for his new territory. This idea was rejected by the king, who argued for it to be named after the fallen admiral instead. And thus, "Pennsylvania" was born. At just 37, William was among the most powerful landowners in all of the British Empire.

A painting depicting Penn and King Charles II

In October 1682, William arrived in America, setting foot on Pennsylvanian soil for the first time. A few dozen Quakers had come along with him, scholars and vagrants alike, all anxious to take part in the pioneering project. Now that he was there, the promise of Pennsylvania was truly unveiled; the enterprising William envisioned an enormous city stretching along the Delaware

River. One of his companions, Thomas Holmes, was appointed the head city planner. Week after week, Holmes trudged through the thick of the woods, mapping out future roads and establishments. Unlike the congested and complicated streets back home, the new city would be constructed in a clean, grid-like pattern, free of walls and dark alleys, which were said to be the breeding grounds of evil.

To achieve this, more territory was required. This would be a challenge on its own, as neighboring villages were already packed with Native American and other European settlers who had been there long before them. William knew that kindness would be the only key to winning the trust of the tentative villagers. He engaged in fair and peaceful negotiations with European settlers, and convinced them to sell their land to him. Soon, Europe was abuzz with rumors of this elysian community, and many more hopped on a boat to join them. From then on, the growing city was known as "Philadelphia."

William's attitude towards the Native Americans was yet another factor that set him apart from other American settlers. In late 1682, William and his companions approached and slowly befriended the Lenape Tribe, who lived by the great river. To demonstrate his commitment to an equal partnership, William devoted his time to learning their language and customs, and he attended their ceremonies with no judgment. In time, the Lenape and the American Quakers arrived at an agreement. The Lenape handed over their land in exchange for a solid price, and their terms were detailed in what is now known as "Penn's Treaty," a document that seemingly symbolized a new era of peace and prosperity between the natives and American settlers. Little did the Lenape know that the written document held nothing but empty words.

In the following years, the persecuted continued to populate Philadelphia, and by 1699, the city had become one of North America's most innovative in the fields of business, science, and education. This, in part, had much to do with the utopian community's unconventional philosophies. The American Quakers believed in an "enlightened penal code." This ensured that prisoners were taught a certain trade during confinement so that they could be reformed and become contributing members of society when released. Following in the footsteps of the British Quakers, boys and girls in Philadelphia received equal education, as Friends believed all deserved equal opportunities in the workforce. This was especially revolutionary in a time when most women were illiterate.

Other than William's benevolence towards the natives, more heads cocked to their sides when he announced that he would not need a military. This seemed especially daring – foolish, even – as European colonies in the New World were extremely vulnerable. Last, but not least, as the "Absolute Proprietor" of Pennsylvania, William encouraged religious freedom not just for the Quakers but to anyone who colored outside the lines of society, as long as their intentions were good and pure.

Friction and Foes

"No pain, no palm; no thorns, no throne; no gall, no glory; no cross, no crown." – William Penn

William's carefully crafted alliance with Tamanend, the Lenape chief who had signed the treaty with him at Shackamaxon, soon soured. The alarmed Tamanend watched as throngs of construction workers invaded the land, swishing their axes and chopping down trees that once stood in the vibrant Lenape forests, to make room for the new city. The chief of the Turtle Clan had been under the impression that William and his men would preserve the land, and he quickly became convinced that these white men were looking to pull one over on him. Hearsay suggested that a dark, ulterior motive lay behind William's sudden camaraderie with the natives – he was planning to herd up the natives and evict them from their own land, as he feared the unfamiliar faces would scare off the myriads of incoming British settlers.

Eventually, the Lenape announced that they no longer wanted anything to do with William. The lamentable tidings deeply wounded the Quaker, who was said to have liked the natives. Most white men of his time vilified the natives as "savages," but William often spoke and wrote highly about the natives. He once said about them, "But in liberality they excel; nothing is too good for their friend. Give them a fine gun, coat, or other thing, it may pass 20 hands before it sticks...[They are] the most merry creatures that live, feast, and dance perpetually; they never have much, nor want much."

The hurdle with the natives was only one of the dozens sprouting up in William's path. In 1684, just 2 years after William's arrival, he would face Lord Baltimore of Maryland head on in a long-lasting territorial dispute. Trouble surfaced when Lord Baltimore came out of the woodwork to claim that he owned several portions of Pennsylvania, and he commanded the Philadelphian settlers to take a hike. William had no choice but to make the 3,000 mile journey back home, where he would work to garner proof for his rightful ownership to the land. At this point, William's old friend, the Duke of York, had risen to the throne as King James II, and he was a monarch both admired and notorious for his support of religious toleration.

King James II

However, in William's absence, the residents of Philadelphia, like mutinous children freed from the supervision of their parents, wreaked havoc. Unruly Philadelphians loitered in caves by the river and crowded in makeshift alleyways that cut through the city. The clean grid layout William so pined for was no more, and even worse, these alleys and cave parties multiplied with round-the-clock gambling, nonstop drinking, and promiscuous sexual activities. It appeared as if the majority of these displaced dissenters with evidently questionable morals had not an inkling of interest in Quakerism or wholesome community living.

When the 55-year-old William returned to Pennsylvania after a 15-year absence, he was confounded by the shocking state of affairs. It was a true fall from grace – Philadelphia's crime and incarceration rates were the highest of all the colonial cities. Prostitutes stalked the streets as canoodling couples posted in every corner showed grossly public displays of affection. Sloppy drunkards drifted from one pub to another in broad daylight. Men, women, and children were shortly fused, and wild, impromptu brawls had become the norm.

Penn in older age

Other American Quakers were dealing with the much more pressing problem of persecution. In Boston, Massachusetts, Quakerism was among the most grievous of crimes. Quaker ministers and authors, like Ann Austin and Mary Fisher, were only some of the many that would feel others' wrath. Far from Pennsylvania, Quakers were spurned as heretics by Bostonian authorities, locked up, and had their works thrown into bonfires. In time, they were released, disgraced, and deported, never allowed to return.

The severity of the punishments depended on the region. Some were luckier than most and were only imprisoned as a warning before they were banished. Others were scourged, scarred for life with branding irons, and suffered other cruel and unusual punishment. Christopher Holder, a Quaker based in New England, had his ears sheared off. More stories of flogging, property confiscation, and eternal banishment sprung forth in New Amsterdam, Rhode Island, and New York. Even the Dutch West India Company despised them, often belittling the "abominable religion."

By the late 17th century, the Quaker paranoia in England had subsided. King James II had been replaced by the co-monarchs King William and Queen Mary, who issued the Toleration Act of 1689. This decree provided religious freedom for Protestant dissenters, barring those who promoted transubstantiation (a measure aimed at the Catholics).

However, as British Quakers reveled in their new freedom, the American Quakers had begun to turn on each other, and it was at this point that a man named George Keith proved pivotal. When Keith, a former dedicated Quaker from Scotland, decided that the Friends had veered too far off course from their original tracks, he deserted the following in early 1691. The Quakers around him, he believed, had become insatiable and morally corrupt, so he took it upon himself to raise his own army, the "Christian Quakers." Keith's small but vicious army of Quaker dissidents began to barge into and obstruct peaceful Quaker meetings. The pacifists did not fight back but defended themselves by latching their doors shut with padlocks. This did little to stop the Christian Quakers, who attacked the padlocks with hatches and broke in anyway, prompting dread and unrest in American Quaker communities.

This nerve-racking tension would carry on for another 2 decades.

Freedom Fighters

"Quakers [are] almost as good as colored. They call themselves 'Friends' and you can trust them every time." – A quote attributed to Harriet Tubman

William Penn was more than just a vigorous visionary. Thomas Jefferson once called him one of the greatest lawmakers to have ever lived. William's first charter, which had been drawn up before he set sail for Pennsylvania, was aptly titled "Frame of Government," and it became the new colony's first ever constitution. On top of permitting absolute religious tolerance and reinforcing traditional British rights, William's laws prevented any other rulers from rising to power, which he feared would endanger the community. William also made sure to include an amending clause, which meant that the charter could be adjusted at any time in the future.

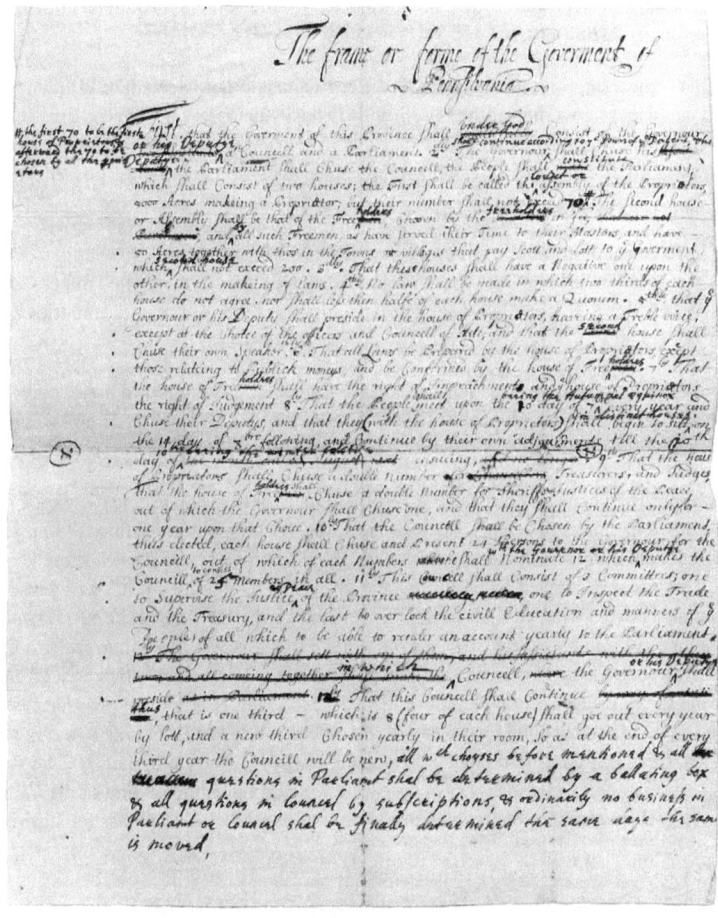

A picture of the first draft of the Frame of Government

On October 28, 1701, a revised version of the constitution, entitled "The Charter of Privileges," otherwise known as the "Charter of Liberties," came into effect. The altered document presented scores of changes that unlocked many new liberties. The charter started off by emphasizing the freedom of worship for all in Pennsylvania. No one was to be "in any case molested or prejudiced" due to "his or their Conscientious persuasion or practice." Land ownership was no longer a requirement for anyone who wished to hold public office. The line between church and state was bolded; no more taxes from here on out could be utilized to support religious institutions.

The most critical of all these changes was the reorganization of legislature. William Markham, the Anglican deputy governor of the Province of Pennsylvania, saw his powers greatly reduced, and he retained only a managerial position. The new legislature was responsible for electing their own leaders and officials, and for establishing their own laws, rendering the governor's voice mute.

Some have gone so far as to assert that this charter was the precursor of American democracy. Modern historians believe that the charter served as a template for the United States Constitution and the Bill of Rights, as well as a basis for legislation for other democratic countries around the world.

Once the charter was approved, William left for England, never to return. Later on, when he became bedridden, his wife, Hannah Callowhill Penn, stepped up to the plate and would head the Pennsylvanian government for 13 years.

Towards the 18th century, the attitude towards Quakerism shifted. Around the world, Quakers became valued members of society, applauded for their numerous contributions to business, science, and human rights. British Quakers, though still shunned from the academic world, built solid reputations as honorable businessmen and traders who not only provided excellent quality goods but also never swindled their customers. Indeed, tany of these Quaker businessmen would play a conductive role in the Industrial Revolution. There was William Allen, an Irish Quaker and the owner of a Plough Court, a reputable pharmaceutical company. Allen created and became the first president of the Pharmaceutical Society, a unified body of pharmacists headed by a committee of 40 that aimed to protect its members, as well as furthering research in the field. Then, there was the Coalbrookdale Company, owned by the Darby family. The steel and iron magnates re-engineered numbers of inventions, including the rebuilding of the traditional furnace. They were also the first to use affordable iron instead of costly brass for steam engine cylinders.

William Allen

Around the same time, Quakers became increasingly active in the fight for human rights. 18th century Quakers made one of the earliest attempts at tackling mental health issues. British Quaker William Tuke, a tea merchant and a known philanthropist, was outraged by the unsanitary and filthy conditions at the York Lunatic Asylum. Knowing that something had to be done, he drummed up donations from Quaker benefactors and opened the Retreat at York in 1796. The staff at the institution was one of the first to be trained in the modern science of psychology. With much persistence, Tuke petitioned for the York asylum to be shut down, and he ultimately succeeded.

American Quakers also played prominent roles in the abolitionist movement. Quakers had always promoted equality and justice for all, but not all lived by the creed. By the late 1680s, there were hundreds of slaves in Pennsylvania, and the number of Quaker slave-owners in

Philadelphia doubled in William's absence. It was Francis Pastorius, the founder of the first German-American settlement in Pennsylvania, who censured them for their immoral practices. Pastorius later convinced other German immigrants to sign the "Germantown Quaker Petition Against Slavery" in 1688, the first abolitionist document in North America.

A relief portrait of Pastorius

It would take several decades before American Quakers took an official stance against slavery. The number of Quaker slave owners had begun to dwindle, but there were still those who refused to forgo the detestable practice. Some defended themselves by claiming that they were blessing their slaves with God's Word, but for John Woolman, a farmer from New Jersey, that was nowhere near enough. Woolman began to raise a stink about slavery in public, arguing that not one principle behind slavery aligned with Christian principles. Slowly, more Quakers agreed with that stance, and they began pitching in to further the movement.

In 1733, the Germantown Quakers included an "opposition to slavery" in their meeting minutes. 43 years later, the Philadelphia Yearly Meeting formally banned its members from owning slaves. It was no coincidence that Philadelphia's most famous Founding Father, Benjamin Franklin, became President of the Pennsylvania Abolitionist Society near the end of his life and advocated strongly for the abolition of slavery, giving several speeches and statements in favor of abolition. Franklin would futilely petition the new American government to end slavery near the end of his life, and the compromises made over slavery at the Constitutional Convention were clearly on his mind when he addressed the other delegates to explain his support for the new Constitution: "I confess that there are several parts of this constitution which I do not at present approve, but I am not sure I shall never approve them: For having lived long, I have experienced many instances of being obliged by better information, or fuller consideration, to change opinions even on important subjects, which I once thought right, but found to be otherwise. It is therefore that the older I grow, the more apt I am to doubt my own judgment, and to pay more respect to the judgment of others.... I doubt too whether any other Convention we can obtain, may be able to make a better Constitution. For when you assemble a number of men to have the advantage of their joint wisdom, you inevitably assemble with those men, all their prejudices, their passions, their errors of opinion, their local interests, and their selfish views. From such an assembly can a perfect production be expected? It therefore astonishes me, Sir, to find this system approaching so near to perfection as it does; and I think it will astonish our enemies, who are waiting with confidence to hear that our councils are confounded like those of the Builders of Babel; and that our States are on the point of separation, only to meet hereafter for the purpose of cutting one another's throats. Thus I consent, Sir, to this Constitution because I expect no better, and because I am not sure, that it is not the best. The opinions I have had of its errors, I sacrifice to the public good. I have never whispered a syllable of them abroad. Within these walls they were born, and here they shall die."

The Quakers also played a critical role in the legendary Underground Railroad. Reverend Samuel Ward, whose parents escaped from Maryland to New Jersey in 1820, explained that "when the slave-catchers came prowling about, the Quakers placed all manners of peaceful obstacles in their way." William Wells Brown, an escaped slave who also worked on the Underground Railroad, supported the sentiment. Brown famously insisted, "No fugitive was ever betrayed by a Quaker."

After the American Civil War, not only would the Quakers help raise hundreds of thousands of dollars in general aid, they constructed collections of schools, universities, and clinics for the freedmen during the Reconstruction years that followed.

Ironically, given the role they played in the nation's most politically charged issue, the Quakers mostly eschewed politics. The Philadelphian Quakers were heavily involved in politics between the 17th and 18th century, and they held the seats for the majority of public office positions in Pennsylvania, but over time, Anglicans, other dissenters, and even some Quakers became steadily disheartened by their government. These explosive tensions came to a head in the Philadelphia Election Riot of 1742. By the 1750s, the Quakers themselves began to realize that their participation in politics contradicted with their religious principles, and chose to cease the tradition. Quakers slowly disappeared from public office, with 1 out of 5 gone by 1775. By the time the American Revolution ended in 1783, the last Quaker had resigned, officially ending the great Holy Experiment.

Modern Quakers

"A good end cannot sanctify evil means; nor must we ever do evil that good may come of it...let us then try what love will do." – William Penn

As the Quakers entered the 19th century, they continued to make progress in scientific and industrial advancement. In 1825, the Pease Family created the Stockton & Darling Railway Company, which made headlines by establishing the first modern railway in the world. Transporting coal to sea ports and other faraway places not only became more efficient, it was now a breeze.

Quaker businessmen were also favored for their philanthropic contributions. The British Quakers were some of the most exceptionally talented chocolatiers in the world, but they would also be cheered on for their goodwill. One such company was Rowntree's, operated by brothers Joseph and Henry Isaac, most known for creating the delectable Smarties chocolates and delightfully crunchy Kit Kat bars. The Rowntree brothers are remembered for providing their workers with some of the best wages and benefits available. Charity foundations in their name have also built schools, learning centers, and low-cost housing for poor families.

Another confectionery mogul was John Cadbury, who opened his first shop at the age of 22. Cadbury started off with a range of tea, coffee, and drinking chocolates. These rich chocolate beverages were considered a luxury at the time, and could only be afforded by the wealthiest families in Birmingham. The capable business shark and advertiser that Cadbury was, he soon transformed the drinking chocolate industry. Equipped with a mortar and pestle, Cadbury created a series of chocolate drinks. These new creations included healthier ingredients designed to counteract the cocoa, but better yet, they were affordable to the masses. As a devout Quaker, he was involved in various campaigns that sought to end poverty, and it became his mission to use tea, coffee, and chocolate as a way to shrink alcoholism, which he believed was a major contributing factor to poverty. Today, the company remains on the 2017 list of the most popular chocolate brands in the world.

Cadbury

Throughout that time, Quakers around the world resumed with their unabated pursuit on human rights. In the early 19th century, Elias Hicks, a traveling Quaker preacher who hailed from New York, wrote a powerful pamphlet against slavery. From then on, more people took heed, and began to consciously avoid products produced through slave labor.

Quaker ministers such as Susan B. Anthony and Lucretia Mott would also join the front lines of abolitionist causes, but at the same time, they fanned the flames for the women's rights campaigns. The Quakers have always been known as feminists, and they played a defining role in the American Women's Suffrage Movement. 5 women, 4 of whom were Quakers, drafted the Declaration of Sentiments, along with 11 other resolutions, demanding that women's voices finally be heard. Just 11 days after the meeting, the movement had attracted a crowd of 300, including 40 men. By the end of the day, 100 were moved enough to sign the declaration. A long and winding road still lay ahead of them, but their tenacity would not falter.

Mott

Anthony

Other Quakers tackled prison reform. Elizabeth Fry and her brother, Joseph John Gurney, were both British Quakers who made waves with their protest parades around town. They called for the elimination of the death penalty and appealed to authorities to improve the conditions of the inmates, who lacked almost all rights. The siblings would later create the Association for the Improvement of Female Prisoners in Newgate, dedicated to protecting the women and children in the prison.

Inevitably, as the Quaker population swelled, disagreements and conflicts worsened, leading to several nasty breakups. There were the Gurneyites, liberal Quakers who disregarded many of Fox's outdated philosophies. There were the Wilburites, conservative Fox fanatics who sought to popularize orthodox Quakerism once more. There were also the Hicksites, named after their leader, Elias Hicks, who left the movement after citing irreconcilable differences regarding slavery and theological views.

Hicks

The 20th century saw more division among the ever-growing Quakers, but that era would also bring about the Quakers' first attempt at coming together as one. In 1920, "liberal" Quakers in London organized a worldwide conference, inviting Friends from various backgrounds for a round of civil discussions and debates. This first version of conferences would fizzle out rather quickly, as they were financially out of reach for most Quakers, but a more fruitful attempt came in the form of the Friends World Committee for Consultation, which was established in 1958.

British Quakers would also be instrumental in war-induced restorations and rescue operations.

After World War I, the Quakers created several foundations centered on veteran support. They would also participate in the Kindertransport operation of 1938-1939, which aspired to provide 10,000 European Jewish children fleeing the Nazis with visas for the UK. In addition to pushing the government for quicker action, hundreds of Quakers welcomed displaced children into their homes.

The growing number of Quakers has continued to invite more controversies, particularly when it comes to their stance on the LGBT community. Unlike the majority of religious sects, liberal Quakers are known supporters of LGBT rights. In certain countries, such as Australia and New Zealand, the overwhelming majority of Quakers pride themselves on their acceptance of people across the sexuality spectrum, and the majority have supported LGBT partnerships. A published quote from the Quakers of Westminster Meeting supports this almost universal Quaker stance: "We affirm the love of God for all people, whatever their sexual orientation...to reject people on the grounds of their sexual behavior is a denial of God's creation."

Modern Quaker factions have been classified into several categories. Liberal Friends practice "unprogrammed" (silent) worship, and lean towards service rather than missionary work. Conservative Friends choose to honor the original Quaker doctrines and philosophies as is; some even still live by the traditional "plain dress" code. Then there are the Evangelical Friends, who believe in the authority of the Bible, often referring to themselves as "churches" instead of "meetings."

Regardless of how they're classified, the Quakers have yet to lose their momentum. Entering the current decade, there were an estimated 210,000 Quakers worldwide.

Online Resources

Other American history titles by Charles River Editors

Other titles about the Quakers on Amazon

Bibliography

Richards, Trisha. "The English Civil Wars and Quaker Persecution." Cornell College. Cornell College, 2004. Web. 13 Feb. 2017. <http://www.cornellcollege.edu/english/Blaugdone/essays/civilwar.htm>.

Editors, Quakers in Britain. "Our history." Quakers in Britain. Religious Society of Friends (Quakers), 2014. Web. 13 Feb. 2017. <https://www.quaker.org.uk/about-quakers/our-history#heading-1>.

Editors, Religious Tolerance. "Christian denominations and homosexuality." Religious Tolerance. Ontario Consultants on Religious Tolerance, 24 Oct. 1998. Web. 13 Feb. 2017. <http://www.religioustolerance.org/hom_quak.htm>.

Editors, ESR. "100 Bible Verses Most Frequently Quoted By Early Quakers." Quaker Bible Index. Earlham School of Religion, 2007. Web. 13 Feb. 2017. <http://www.wutka.com/download/qbn.pdf>.

Editors, Religious Tolerance. "Quaker beliefs and practices." Religious Tolerance. Ontario Consultants on Religious Tolerance, 2009. Web. 13 Feb. 2017. <http://www.religioustolerance.org/quaker2.htm>.

Editors, New World Encylopedia. "Quakers." New World Encylopedia. MediaWiki, 18 June 2015. Web. 13 Feb. 2017. <https://www.newworldencyclopedia.org/entry/Quakers>.

Editors, QIC. "Branches of Friends Today." Quaker Information Center. Earlham School of Religion, 26 May 2011. Web. 13 Feb. 2017. <http://www.quakerinfo.org/quakerism/branches/today>.

Editors, Brit Politics Library. "Causes of the Civil War." Brit Politics Library. Britology, Ltd., 2009. Web. 13 Feb. 2017. <http://www.britpolitics.co.uk/causes-of-the-civil-war>.

Editors, Biography.Com. "Mary Tudor Biography." Biography. A&E Television Networks, LLC, 2011. Web. 13 Feb. 2017. <http://www.biography.com/people/mary-tudor-9401296>.

Hughes, Richard. "The Ears of William Prynne." History Today. History Today, Ltd., Mar. 2008. Web. 13 Feb. 2017. <http://www.historytoday.com/richard-hughes/ears-william-prynne>.

Editors, BCW Project. "The Second Bishops' War, 1640." British Civil Wars Project. UK Battlefields Resource Centre, 24 Nov. 2010. Web. 13 Feb. 2017. <http://bcw-project.org/military/bishops-wars/second-bishops-war>.

Trueman, C. N. "James I and Royal Revenue." The History Learning Site. The History Learning Site, Ltd., 16 Aug. 2016. Web. 13 Feb. 2017. <http://www.historylearningsite.co.uk/stuart-england/james-i-and-royal-revenue/>.

Editors, Biography.Com. "Charles II of England." Biography. A&E Television Networks, LLC, 2011. Web. 13 Feb. 2017. <http://www.biography.com/people/charles-ii-of-england-39462>.

Rivers, Isabel, and David L. Wykes. "Protestant Dissent." The Queen Mary Centre for Religion and Literature in English. Queen Mary University of London, 2016. Web. 13 Feb. 2017. <http://www.qmulreligionandliterature.co.uk/research/the-dissenting-academies-project/protestant-dissent/>.

Gatiss, Lee. "THE GREAT EJECTION." Evangelical Times. SCK Webworks, Ltd., Aug. 2012. Web. 13 Feb. 2017. <http://www.evangelical-times.org/archive/item/5632/Historical/-THE-GREAT-EJECTION---The-Great-Ejection-of-1662/>.

Heron, Alastair. "Quaker Origins." Mid-Essex Quakers. Chelmsford Quakers, 1997. Web. 13 Feb. 2017. <http://www.midessexquakers.org.uk/quaker-origins.php>.

Editors, The Famous People. "George Fox Biography." The Famous People. The Famous People, Ltd., 2007. Web. 13 Feb. 2017. <http://www.thefamouspeople.com/profiles/george-fox-4791.php>.

Graves, Dan. "#406: GEORGE FOX AND THE QUAKERS." Christian History Institute. Christian History Institute, 2010. Web. 13 Feb. 2017. <https://www.christianhistoryinstitute.org/study/module/george-fox/>.

Editors, Healing and Revival. ""The Life of God is the Light of Men"." Healing and Revival. Healing and Revival Press, 2004. Web. 13 Feb. 2017. <http://healingandrevival.com/BioGFox.htm>.

Graves, Dan, MSL. "George Fox, founder of the Quakers." Christianity.Com. Salem Web Network, 2017. Web. 13 Feb. 2017. <http://www.christianity.com/church/church-history/timeline/1601-1700/george-fox-founder-of-the-quakers-11630109.html>.

Walvin, James, and John Murray. "The Quakers Money and Morals." The New York Times. The New York Times Company, 1997. Web. 13 Feb. 2017. <http://www.nytimes.com/books/first/w/walvin-quakers.html>.

Gaultiere, Bill. "All Articles Christ the Inward Teacher (From the Journal of George Fox)." Soul Shepherding. Soul Shepherding, Ltd., 9 Feb. 2015. Web. 13 Feb. 2017. <http://www.soulshepherding.org/2015/02/christ-inward-teacher-journal-george-fox/>.

Editors, BBC. "Quakers - the Religious Society of Friends." BBC . BBC, 3 July 2009. Web. 13 Feb. 2017. <http://www.bbc.co.uk/religion/religions/christianity/subdivisions/quakers_1.shtml>.

Editors, UK Wells. "George Fox." UK Wells. WordPress, 2013. Web. 14 Feb. 2017. <http://ukwells.org/revivalists/george-fox/>.

Cavendish, Richard. "The founder of the Quakers died on January 13th 1691." History Today. History Today, Ltd., 2015. Web. 14 Feb. 2017. <http://www.historytoday.com/richard-cavendish/george-fox-dies-london>.

Editors, West Hill Friends. "Valiant Sixty." West Hill Friends. West Hill Friends Church, 2008. Web. 14 Feb. 2017. <http://www.westhillsfriends.org/QVWv60.html>.

Editors, West Richmond Friends. "Quotations from Margaret Fell." West Richmond Friends. West Richmond Friends Church, 2009. Web. 14 Feb. 2017. <http://westrichmondfriends.org/Fell.htm>.

Editors, Jesus Army. "THE VALIANT SIXTY." Jesus Army. Jesus Fellowship Life Trust, Ltd. , 24 July 2006. Web. 14 Feb. 2017. <http://jesus.org.uk/blog/radical-christian-history/valiant-sixty>.

Editors, NPS. "Women in the Quaker Meeting." National Park Service Iowa. National Park Service, U.S. Department of the Interior, 22 June 2010. Web. 14 Feb. 2017. <https://www.nps.gov/heho/learn/historyculture/women-in-the-quaker-faith.htm>.

Editors, Quakers in the World. "Margaret Fell." Quakers in the World. Joseph Rowntree Charitable Trust, 2010. Web. 14 Feb. 2017. <http://www.quakersintheworld.org/quakers-in-action/14>.

Editors, US History. "The Life of Margaret Fell." US History. Independence Hall Association, 4 July 1995. Web. 14 Feb. 2017. <http://www.ushistory.org/penn/margaret_fell.htm>.

Densmore, Christopher. "Radical Quaker Women and the Early Women's Rights Movement." Quakers & Slavery Conference. Friends Historical Library at Swarthmore College, 2015. Web. 14 Feb. 2017. <http://trilogy.brynmawr.edu/speccoll/quakersandslavery/commentary/themes/radical_quaker_women.php>.

Editors, Quakers in the World. "The Holy Experiment, in Pennsylvania." Quakers in the World. Joseph Rowntree Charitable Trust, 2010. Web. 14 Feb. 2017. <http://www.visitcumbria.com/sl/swarthmoor-hall/>.

Editors, Biography.Com. "William Penn." Biography. A&E Television Networks, LLC, 2013. Web. 14 Feb. 2017. <http://www.biography.com/people/william-penn-9436869#synopsis>.

Newman, Andrew. "Treaty of Shackamaxon." The Encyclopedia of Greater Philadelphia. Rutgers-Camden Digital Studies Center, 22 Nov. 2013. Web. 15 Feb. 2017. <http://philadelphiaencyclopedia.org/archive/treaty-of-shackamaxon-2/>.

Baker, Mick. "Tribal Leaders: Head Chief Tamanend the Affable of the Lenape." The History Files. Kessler Associates, 20 May 2016. Web. 15 Feb. 2017. <http://www.historyfiles.co.uk/FeaturesAmericas/NorthNativeTribalLeaders01_Tamanend.htm>.

Penn, William. "William Penn Describes the Lenni-Lenape Indians of Pennsylvania." Herb - Social History for Every Classroom. American Social History Productions, Inc., 2016. Web. 15 Feb. 2017. <https://herb.ashp.cuny.edu/items/show/1465>.

Cody, Edward J. "THE PRICE OF PERFECTION: THE IRONY OF GEORGE KEITH." Portland State University. Portland State University Library, 2005. Web. 15 Feb. 2017. <https://journals.psu.edu/phj/article/viewFile/23586/23355>.

McFerran, Noel S. "Toleration Act, 1689." The Jacobite Heritage. Noel S. McFerran, 26 Oct. 2003. Web. 15 Feb. 2017. <http://www.jacobite.ca/documents/1689toleration.htm>.

Editors, HSP. "William Penn's Charter of Privileges." Historical Society of Pennsylvania. Historical Society of Pennsylvania, 2012. Web. 15 Feb. 2017. <https://hsp.org/education/unit-plans/william-penns-charter-of-privileges>.

Ries, Linda A. "Pennsylvania Charter of Privileges." The Encyclopedia of Greater Philadelphia. Rutgers-Camden Digital Studies Center, 2016. Web. 15 Feb. 2017. <http://philadelphiaencyclopedia.org/archive/pennsylvania-charter-of-privileges/>.

Editors, ALLI. "Frame of Government." American Law & Legal Information. Net Industries, 2005. Web. 16 Feb. 2017. <http://law.jrank.org/pages/11668/Frame-Government.html>.

Editors, Quakers in the World. "William Allen." Quakers in the World. Joseph Rowntree Charitable Trust, 2010. Web. 16 Feb. 2017. <http://www.quakersintheworld.org/quakers-in-action/284/William-Allen>.

Editors, BBC. "William Tuke (1732 - 1822)." BBC . BBC, 2014. Web. 16 Feb. 2017. <http://www.bbc.co.uk/history/historic_figures/tuke_william.shtml>.

Densmore, Christopher. "Quakers and the Underground Railroad: Myths and Realities." Quakers & Slavery Conference. Friends Historical Library at Swarthmore College, 2014. Web. 16 Feb. 2017. <http://trilogy.brynmawr.edu/speccoll/quakersandslavery/commentary/organizations/underground_railroad.php>.

Editors, BGCS. "1688 Germantown Quaker Petition Against Slavery." Black German Cultural Society. WordPress, 24 Feb. 2016. Web. 16 Feb. 2017. <http://afrogermans.us/1688-germantown-quaker-petition-against-slavery/>.

Editors, History Channel. "THE QUAKERS." History Channel. A&E Television Networks, LLC, 2015. Web. 16 Feb. 2017. <http://www.history.com/topics/quakers>.

Editors, RPS. "The History of the Royal Pharmaceutical Society ." The Royal Pharmaceutical Society. Museum of the Royal Pharmaceutical Society, 2015. Web. 17 Feb. 2017. <https://www.rpharms.com/museum-pdfs/history-of-the-society.pdf>.

Editors, GG. "Coalbrookdale Co." Grace's Guide to British Industrial History. Grace's Guide, Ltd., 24 Mar. 2016. Web. 17 Feb. 2017. <http://www.gracesguide.co.uk/Coalbrookdale_Co>.

Editors, AWF. "My favorite Quaker quotes." Are We Friends. WordPress, 21 Apr. 2014. Web. 17 Feb. 2017. <https://arewefriends.wordpress.com/2014/04/21/my-favorite-quaker-quotes/>.

Editors, Quakers in the World. "The Pease Family." Quakers in the World. Joseph Rowntree Charitable Trust, 2010. Web. 17 Feb. 2017. <http://www.quakersintheworld.org/quakers-in-action/360>.

Jackson, Peter. " How did Quakers conquer the British sweet shop?" BBC News. BBC, 20 Jan. 2010. Web. 17 Feb. 2017. <http://news.bbc.co.uk/2/hi/uk_news/magazine/8467833.stm>.

Editors, Cadbury. "The Story of Cadbury." Cadbury. Mondelez Australia Property, Ltd., 2014. Web. 17 Feb. 2017. <https://www.cadbury.com.au/about-cadbury/the-story-of-cadbury.aspx>.

Editors, TTM. "Top 10 Most Popular Chocolate Brands in The World." Trending Top Most. Trending Top Most, Ltd., Sept. 2016. Web. 17 Feb. 2017. <http://www.trendingtopmost.com/worlds-popular-list-top-10/2017-2018-2019-2020-2021/foods/best-selling-chocolate-brands-world-usa-india/>.

Taylor, Gordon Rattray . "Mediaeval Sexual Behaviour." Our Civilisation. P Atkinson, 30 Nov. 2016. Web. 17 Feb. 2017. <http://www.ourcivilisation.com/smartboard/shop/taylorgr/sxnhst/chap2.htm>.

Tuke, Henry. Memoirs of the Life of George Fox . N.p.: Forgotten , 2016. Print.

Ingle, H. Larry. First among Friends: George Fox and the Creation of Quakerism. N.p.: Oxford U Press, 1996. Print.

Fox, George, and Henry J. Cadbury. The Journal of George Fox. N.p.: Friends United Press, 2006. Print.

Kunze, Bonnelyn Young. Margaret Fell and the Rise of Quakerism. N.p.: Stanford Univ Press, 1994. Print.

Miller, D. Douglas. Drumore Quakers Precious Habitation: A 200-Year History of Drumore Friends Meetinghouse and Cemetery. Ed. Kris Miller. N.p.: Xlibris US, 2016. Print.

Ferrett, Andrew, and Devon McReynolds. "In Penn's Shadow (1680-1720) ." Philadelphia: The Great Experiment. History Making Productions. 4 Sept. 2014. Television.

Free Books by Charles River Editors

We have brand new titles available for free most days of the week. To see which of our titles are currently free, click on this link.

Discounted Books by Charles River Editors

We have titles at a discount price of just 99 cents everyday. To see which of our titles are currently 99 cents, click on this link.

Made in United States
Troutdale, OR
11/29/2023